SUPER-CHARGED!

TRUCK AND TRACTOR PULLERS

BY

Rosemary Grimm

PUBLISHED BY

CRESTWOOD HOUSE

Mankato, MN, U.S.A.

CIP

LIBRARY OF CONGRESS CATALOGING IN PUBLICATION DATA

Grimm, Rosemary.
   Truck and tractor pullers.
   (Super-Charged!)
   Includes index.
   SUMMARY: Describes the history, equipment, safety rules, contests, and other aspects of truck and tractor pulling competition.
   1. Tractor driving—Competitions—Juvenile literature. 2. Truck driving—Competitions—Juvenile literature. [1. Tractor driving—Competitions. 2. Truck driving—Competitions] I. Title.
TL233.3.G75   1988   796.7   87-30592
ISBN 0-89686-358-1

International Standard Book Number:	Library of Congress Catalog Card Number:
0-89686-358-1	87-30592

CREDITS

Cover: U.S. Hot Rod Association
Art Arfons: 22, 27
Globe Photos, Inc.: 7
FPG International: (William R. Wilson) 8; (Thomas Zimmerman) 20, 34-35
SRO: 4-5, 13, 21, 25, 26, 30-31, 33, 38, 40, 43
NTPA: 10-11, 12, 15, 16-17, 18, 19, 28-29, 36, 41, 44

Produced by Carnival Enterprises.

CRESTWOOD HOUSE

Box 3427, Mankato, MN, U.S.A. 56002

TABLE OF CONTENTS

A pulling contest is always exciting!

GOING FOR
THE FULL PULL

The powerful roar of the five revved-up engines of the truck puller turns all heads toward the starting line. On this clear night, in front of thousands of

spectators, the driver will test his truck's strength. All those days of welding, hammering, drilling, and polishing are over. His machine is in top form.

The green flag is up! The 5,000-horsepower puller strains to pull weights to the end of the track. The noise throughout the stadium is deafening. The driver noses his puller closer to the end line. The muddy track does not help the truck at all. The wheels spin as they search for traction. Slowly, slowly the puller inches forward. The noise of all five engines at maximum power is almost too loud now. The driver holds his breath until the end of the pull.

He's made it! His truck has pulled the sled the entire length of the track! "Full Pull! Full Pull!" chants the audience. The judges mark down this impressive display of strength: 35,000 pounds (15,875 kilograms) pulled 300 feet (91 meters). The driver turns off his engines and makes a quick check of his equipment. Nothing is seriously damaged, despite the great strain on his puller. It's time to celebrate!

THE HISTORY OF PULLERS

The sport of truck and tractor pulling was not always this exciting. The stadiums, lights, large audiences, and awesome power are recent additions to the sport. The early days of pulling were much quieter.

Farmers have always prided themselves on having the strongest and healthiest livestock. In the 1800's strong, healthy farm animals were needed to pull plows and wagons. The early farmers held contests to see whose horse could pull the most weight or

This tractor may look ordinary—but it's powerful!

whose bull could pull a heavy rock the farthest.

Later, farmers began using tractors instead of livestock for plowing their fields. The farmers fixed up their tractors to pull heavier loads. At county fairs in the 1920's, farmers would get together to look at each other's farm equipment. Friendly tests of strength between these farmers marked the beginning of tractor pulls.

It wasn't until the 1930's, however, that the first pulling contest was officially organized. Those first pulling contests, which were called "tug" pulls, were simple tests of strength. A flat steel slab was loaded

A driver takes his puller to its limit.

with rocks, sandbags, and concrete blocks. A driver hooked up his tractor to the slab. If he could pull the weight ten feet (three meters), he could stay in the contest. If not, he'd have to wait until the next contest to test his tractor's strength.

After the first round, more and more rocks and

sandbags were loaded onto the slab. The drivers kept testing their tractors and more weight was added. Finally, there would be only one tractor left that could pull the weight. That tractor was declared the winner.

For the next 30 years, tractor pulling contests didn't change much. But competitions began to feature truck pullers as well. Then in the 1960's, the steel slab was replaced by a "step on" sled. The sled was still a flat piece of steel. But instead of piling on rocks and sandbags, men jumped on the sled to add weight.

Before a pull, volunteers from the audience would line up on the track at ten-foot (three-meter) intervals. A truck or tractor was hooked up to the flat sled and began its pull down the track. As the sled passed the volunteers, they would jump onto it, one at a time, adding their weight.

Shortly after the "step on" sled was invented, drivers started making their tractor and truck pullers more powerful. The pullers had more horsepower now and needed heavier weights. It was getting too dangerous to jump on the moving sled!

The sleds used today were invented to meet the needs of the stronger truck and tractor pullers. They are safer. They also can increase the weight automatically during a contest. The more powerful sleds challenged the more powerful truck and tractor pullers that were suddenly popping up everywhere!

Truck pullers are only allowed one engine.

TRUCK PULLERS

The biggest difference between truck pullers and tractor pullers is that truck pullers are allowed only one engine. The engine that was in the truck when

it was bought, however, will not be the one used in the pulling contest. A driver will modify his truck until it is a roaring power puller (to modify is to increase the power). Drivers spend thousands of dollars to add a powerful engine to their trucks.

A two-wheel-drive puller has to depend on its large back tires for power.

Truck pullers are either four-wheel or two-wheel drive. In a four-wheel-drive truck, all four wheels receive power from the engine. Four-wheel-drive trucks are the only pulling vehicles that use all four wheels in a contest.

In a two-wheel-drive truck, only two wheels (either the front or the back) receive power. Two-wheel-drive trucks are the newest addition to truck pulling. They have small front tires and large back

Funny Car pullers can be as powerful as any other puller.

tires. In a pull, the back tires receive all the power from the engine and the front tires are lifted off the ground.

Some drivers have added funny car bodies to their two-wheel-drive trucks. These two-wheel-drive sport vehicles were introduced in 1986. Their tires are larger than regular two-wheel- or four-wheel-drive trucks, but are still not as large as the tractor pullers' tires!

TRACTOR PULLERS

The powerful, brightly-colored tractors seen in today's pulls started out as ordinary farm machines. When a farmer had a heavier load to pull, he would modify the engine to give it more power. These new tractor engines signaled the birth of the modified class in tractor pulling. In the 1960's, automobile engines were mounted in the tractor frames. Some drivers even experimented with airplane engines and tank motors. More pulling power is what drivers and mechanics strive for — no matter what!

Modified tractors don't really look like regular farm tractors. They have rear tires and a single seat like a tractor, but that is where the resemblance ends. The long, low body and small front wheels make them look more like dragsters than tractors. Even though truck pullers are allowed only one engine, modified tractors can have up to six! Modifieds have larger fuel pumps and anything else "larger" that will give them more pulling power. And like any racing vehicle, these pullers constantly need new parts. A driver might spend $40,000 to buy modified parts for his special machine.

Smaller modified tractors are called Minis. They are less than eight feet (two meters) long and have only one engine. Minis are difficult to drive — they have high horsepower, but very small frames.

14

Minis are smaller modified tractors.

Drivers must keep a steady hand on the steering wheel to prevent the front end from zig-zagging down the pulling field.

Minis are difficult to drive—but can pull a lot!

17

Pro Stock tractors are nicknamed "Smokers."

Super Stock tractors have super strength!

Pro Stock and Super Stock tractors look more like regular farm machines. But don't let their looks fool you! Underneath their normal-looking frame is an engine that can pull thousands of pounds down the track. Pro Stock tractors have large rear tires and fancy paint jobs. These tractors are often called "smokers" because of the clouds of smoke that always trail behind them as they strain to pull the weights.

Pro Stocks are known for their large rear tires.

Because they sit so close to the pullers' engines, drivers wear fire retardant suits.

SAFETY FEATURES

With all that horsepower, a truck or tractor engine can be a dangerous piece of equipment. Drivers take extra safety precautions when they modify their vehicles.

In most pulling contests, a fire extinguisher is required in the cockpit or cab. The extinguisher must

Tractor pullers come in many shapes and sizes.

be within easy reach of the driver. If a driver can stop a small engine fire right away, he'll reduce his chances of getting seriously hurt — and save thousands of dollars in future repairs. Another safety rule requires drivers to have a fire wall between them and the engine. A fire wall is a fireproof piece of metal that blocks the spread of any fire that might start in the engine area. And although fire-retardant suits are not required for all contest classes, many drivers feel safer having this extra protection.

Other basic equipment used in pulling contests are helmets, lap belts, and shoulder straps. For added safety, the windshield and windows of a pulling vehicle are made of safety glass or plexiglass. These special materials won't shatter when hit with flying rocks.

PREPARING A PULLING TRACK

Thousands of people each year attend truck and tractor pulling contests. Some contests have filled 70,000-seat stadiums. Pulling contests are much louder than rock concerts — sometimes earplugs are sold at the stadium!

Most pulling contests are held in arenas used for football, baseball, or basketball games. The playing surfaces are not at all equipped to handle the mud-splattering pullers. Preparing for a three-day pulling event takes several days and a lot of hard work.

One week before the contest, work crews lay plywood boards and plastic sheets over the stadium's surface. The boards and sheets will protect the original surface from the dirt and mud that will make up the pulling surface.

A few days later, 4,000 cubic yards (3,058 cubic meters) of dirt are brought to the stadium. That's about 750 dump truck loads! The dirt will make a track that is 300 feet (91 meters) long and 35 feet (10 meters) wide.

As the track is being prepared, extra ushers, ticket takers, and security people are hired. Since pulling contests draw big crowds, many people are needed to make the event run smoothly.

Some sponsors pay as much as $250,000 to prepare a stadium for a big pulling event. The money is well-spent, however. When the stadium track is finished it will last throughout all the pulling events. After the contest, work crews can return the stadium to its original state in just 12 hours!

THE PULLING CONTEST

The object of a pulling contest is to hook a vehicle to an ever-increasing load and see how far down a track the puller can drag the weight before losing traction — or killing the engine. If a puller can get the weight to the end of the track, he has made a full pull. If more than one puller completes a full pull, a pull-off determines the winner.

In a pull-off, more and more weight is added to the sled until only one truck and one tractor can pull the weight the farthest. A pulling contest settles any argument about whose truck or tractor has the most sheer pulling power!

All pulling vehicles must be registered with the

A pulling track is prepared a week before the big event.

When the green flag signals ''Go,'' a puller must be ready.

Last-minute adjustments are made on this modified tractor.

judges before the contest. The drivers enter their vehicles into different classes depending on the horsepower and weight of their truck or tractor.

At registration, drivers pick a number to determine their pulling position. If a driver develops a mechanical problem after he registers, he will be allowed to drop to the last pulling position. Otherwise, his puller must be ready to go when his position is called.

Instead of front wheels, a sled has a steel skid plate.

An hour before the pulling contest begins, a drivers' meeting is usually held. At the meeting, the judges show drivers the track boundaries and review safety rules. The drivers are told where they must be when it is their time to pull. After the drivers' meeting, final preparations for pulling can begin!

THE SLED

As the drivers prepare their pulling vehicles, the contest officials prepare the weight transfer machine (known as the sled). The sled supplies the ever-increasing load that will challenge each puller. The

As the sled's weights move forward, more strain is put on the skid plate.

modern sled looks a lot like a truck trailer. It has a
long flat bed and huge rear tires. But, instead of front
tires, the sled has a steel skid plate. The skid plate is
a flat piece of steel attached to the underside of the
trailer. The sled also features huge, moveable weights
on its trailer bed. The sled itself can weigh 20,000

pounds (9,071 kilograms) and may carry 15,000 pounds (6,803 kilograms) of weights!

At the beginning of the pull, the weights are located right above the sled's tires. There is no pressure on the skid plate, so it is off the ground. As the truck or tractor pulls the sled forward, the sled's weights also move forward — from the back of the trailer to the front. As the weights get closer to the front skid plate, the plate is pressed against the ground. The faster the puller moves, the faster the weights apply pressure to the skid plate.

Eventually, the weights are directly above the skid plate. They are now putting maximum pressure on the plate, pressing it firmly to the ground. The puller must use all its power to keep the sled moving in spite of the heavy load.

SLED OPERATORS

During a pulling contest, the sled carries weights, the skid plate, and a sled operator. The sled operator sits on the top or back of the sled and makes sure the machine is operating correctly. If the puller runs into trouble or drives out of bounds, the sled operator can stop the sled. He even has a separate "kill" switch that lets him turn off the puller's engines in an emergency.

A sled operator must be aware of possible trouble spots. Stones from the pulling track can fly into the audience. Loose equipment on the puller or sled can endanger the driver. The operator must know when to stop a pull.

Mud flaps and a plexiglass shield on the back of the sled protect the operator from mud and rocks.

A sled operator hooks up the puller to the weight transfer machine.

There are lights on the back of the sled that the operator controls. A red light means the sled is still being prepared. A green light means it is ready to pull.

The operator's most important job, though, is preparing the sled before a pull. The operator studies the length of the pulling track, the track surface (wet, muddy, or dry), and the type of puller. Then he adjusts the weights to meet all conditions. Now the sled is ready!

At the beginning of a pull, the weights are on top of the sled's back wheels.

The first puller tests track conditions and sled operation.

PULLERS TO THEIR POSITION!

When the green light signals the start of a pull, the truck or tractor must begin the pull within three minutes. The driver steps on the gas and gets off to a fast start. He wants to "stay ahead of the sled," which means he wants to pull faster than the weights moving toward the skid plate. The weights soon catch up, but if he's quick, the driver can gain valuable seconds of pulling power. In a pulling contest, time is not important. What's important is how long the puller can continue to pull.

The first contestant in a pulling contest is the test puller. His truck or tractor puller tests the track and the sled for the other pullers. The test puller determines if the sled operators need to adjust the sled or if more dirt needs to be added to the track. When the test is complete, the test puller pulls his first load. If the test puller, or any other contestant, does not pull the sled to the 75-foot (22-meter) line on the track, he is given a second try. The second attempt is the driver's last chance to stay in the contest.

With all that power straining the truck or tractor puller, the driver must control lift. Lift occurs when a puller's front end rises off the ground as the weight on the sled increases. If there is too much weight on the front of the puller (from the engines and other equipment) the puller "plows" — it can't lift off the ground. If a driver wants to stay in the contest, he removes any extra equipment. The driver cannot

To complete a full pull, a driver must know how to control lift.

stop lift, but if he can control it, he has a better chance of making a full pull.

Ideally, a driver wants to get off the starting line fast and let his puller lift off the ground. Then he wants to continue pulling without braking until he reaches the end of the track.

A driver is sometimes forced to brake if his puller veers to one side or heads out of bounds, but this can waste precious time.

JUDGES AND FLAGMEN

In all official pulling contests, judges measure the length of a pull. Before a pull, they meet with the drivers and inspect pullers. Flagmen signal the start of a pull and mark pulling distances.

Each class of pullers has a certain legal weight. Before the pull, judges weigh the vehicles after oil and gasoline have been added. The puller is not allowed to pull if it is 50 pounds (22 kilograms) over the weight limit for its class.

The flagmen work with the sled operators to make sure the sled is ready before they wave the green "go" flag. A driver is disqualified if he begins his pull before the green flag is raised.

After the driver has pulled the sled's weight as far as he can, a lineman measures the length of the pull from the starting line to the front of the sled's skid plate. The measurement is brought to the judges who calculate which driver has pulled the farthest. If a driver has pulled less than 75 feet (22 meters), he is given a second try.

After all vehicles have pulled, the judges take a few minutes to double-check their calculations. Then the winner for each class of pullers is announced. Trophies and prize money are presented to the smiling, proud drivers. Throughout the year, other awards are given to the most improved drivers and to the best mechanics.

Flagmen tell the drivers when it is safe to begin a pull.

THE DRIVERS

Truck and tractor drivers come from all occupations. They aren't all farmers or mechanics. Most puller drivers are, however, able to fix their own vehicles. They've worked long and hard on their pullers and are usually able to fix small, last-minute problems.

Art Arfons maneuvers his **Green Monster**.

Within the sport of truck and tractor pulling, a driver is independent. Any driver can pull in any contest as long as he has pre-registered. Drivers must be at least 18 years old or have a parent's or guardian's written consent.

Art Arfons from Akron, Ohio, is a popular driver. He designed and built "The Green Monster" tractor, a mighty machine powered by two jet helicopter engines! The Green Monster puts out a 15-foot (4.5-meter) flame as its engines roar. After 20 years of drag racing, Art decided to try tractor pulling. He gave the sport its first turbine-powered tractor.

Art's daughter, 20-year-old Dusty Arfons, is one of the youngest female tractor pullers in the country. She started out as a member of Art's crew and learned much about the sport of tractor pulling from her dad. Her tractor, "The Dragon Lady," has over 1,500 horsepower—now Dusty competes against her dad in the same class. Dusty hopes someday to be the first female national champion tractor puller.

Jim Brockman became interested in pulling after donating a tractor for use at a local pull. "The noise and excitement of the pulling got into my blood," Jim said. "I parked the tractor at the 200-foot mark so I would have a good seat."

Jim's pride and joy are his two-wheel-drive trucks named "Inlaw" and "Outlaw." Inlaw is a 1949 panel truck and Outlaw is a 1941 Dodge.

*Dusty Arfons' **Dragon Lady** puts out a huge flame as it pulls the sled.*

Jim Brockman's two-wheel-drive roars down the track.

MICRO MINI TRACTOR PULLING

Nothing can compare to the excitement and noise of a stadium full of people watching a tractor pull. But some people like to have that excitement in miniature. These people "drive" their model-sized truck and tractor pullers across a table top! Table-top pulling is done on a 15-foot (4.5-meter) table. The pullers are either modified toy truck or tractors or kit-built pullers with lots of detail. The pullers are powered by model airplane engines or electric motors.

As with larger vehicles, these micro mini pullers are classed as Modifieds, four-wheel, and two-wheel drive. Weight classes range from three to six pounds. These "little screamers" can pull up to 350 pounds (158 kilograms) of weight!

This unique pulling sport costs much less than the full-sized version. A damaged engine in a micro mini puller costs about $20. With large pullers, a driver would need $20,000 to fix an engine. Table-top pulling can be set up anywhere, and no special week-long preparations are needed. Many county fairs sponsor this type of pulling along with "real" pulling contests.

A GROWING MOTORSPORT

Truck and tractor pulling is one of the fastest-growing motorsports in the country. A wheel-spinning, dirt-flying pull can excite just about anyone. Truck and tractor pulling series and championships are becoming better organized. And, as more and more pulling contests are held, more and more people are becoming fans. This unique display of power will continue to grow in popularity!

FOR MORE INFORMATION

For more information on truck and tractor pullers and pulling contests write to:
SRO/Pace Promotions
590 West Grand Avenue
Suite C
Hot Springs, AR 71901

National Tractor Pullers Association
6969 Worthington-Galena Road
Suite L-1000
Worthington, OH 43085

GLOSSARY/INDEX

FOUR-WHEEL DRIVE 12, 13, 45 — *In a vehicle with four-wheel drive, all four wheels receive power from the engine.*

FULL PULL 6, 24, 38 — *During competition, pulling a sled the entire length of the track.*

HORSEPOWER 5, 9, 14, 21, 27, 42 — *The unit for measuring the power of an engine.*

KILL SWITCH 32 — *A switch that automatically shuts off the engine if a puller becomes unhooked from the sled.*

LIFT 37, 38 — *A puller's front end rising off the ground during a pulling contest.*

MODIFIED 11, 14, 21, 44, 45 — *Changing a puller's engine to make it more powerful.*

PLOWING 37 — *Too much weight on the front of the puller; the puller will not lift off the ground.*

PULL OFF 24 — *Determines the winner of a pulling contest if more than one puller completes a full pull.*

SECOND ATTEMPT 37, 39 — *If, on the first try, a puller doesn't pull the sled to the 75-foot (22-meter) line, the puller can try again.*

SKID PLATE 30, 31, 32, 37, 39 — *A flat piece of steel located under the front end of the sled. As the sled's weights move on top of the skid plate, the plate presses against the ground and makes the puller work harder to pull the sled.*

GLOSSARY/INDEX

SLED 7, 24, 29, 30, 31, 32, 33, 37 — *The weight transfer machine.*

SMOKERS 19 — *The nickname for Super Stock tractors.*

TEST PULLER 37 — *The first puller of each class to check the sled gear and weights.*

TWO-WHEEL DRIVE 12, 13, 42, 45 — *In a vehicle with two-wheel drive, only two wheels (either the front or back) receive power from the engine.*

TURBINE 42 — *An engine using explosive fuel to drive rotary fan blades that create the turning power of the engine. Turbine engines are commonly used in jet aircraft.*